W9-AHZ-216

Jonah:

The Man Whose God and Heart Were Too Small

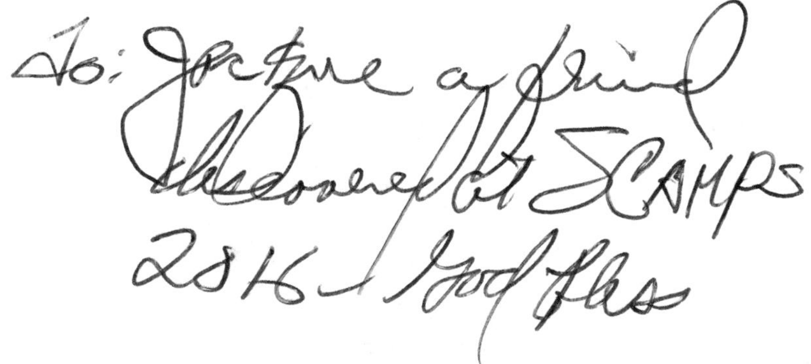

Dr. Dean Cook

AuthorHouse™
1663 Liberty Drive
Bloomington, IN 47403
www.authorhouse.com
Phone: 1 (800) 839-8640

Published by AuthorHouse 02/23/2015

ISBN: 978-1-4969-6286-7 (sc)
ISBN: 978-1-4969-6285-0 (e)

Library of Congress Control Number: 2015900398

Print information available on the last page.

CONTENTS

PREFACE

It is interesting to me how people can hear a sermon on a Sunday morning and lock onto an illustration the preacher gives and miss the real point of the sermon altogether. This, I am afraid, is often true in our hearing and thinking about the book of Jonah. We tend to get "hooked" on the fish and miss the real storyline that runs throughout the book. This book is not about the fish, although God's use of this creature adds humor to the story and reminds us that He is a very creative God. The story is really about the prophet and how his view of the world differs from God's. This difference is highlighted when God asks him to do something he doesn't want to do – namely to go preach God's message to Bloody Nineveh. This confrontation exposes Jonah's real heart and view of God. Many of us, like Jonah, have our understanding of God and the world shaped by our culture, our religious tradition, our nation, and our prejudices. The result is that we can end up worshipping and serving the god we want, rather than the God who is.

Because of His love for us, God will confront this falsehood in us as he did in Jonah. Jonah responded with anger, disrespect, and even disobedience by trying to flee from his calling and his God. The book is about how God in love and mercy pursued Jonah from a storm to a fish to Nineveh and finally to a crude shelter. There Jonah sits pouts and pleads to die because God is too good and too kind. The book examines our faith. Have we, too, adopted a narrow god that we want rather than the great and loving God who is? Is God pursuing us even now, calling us to abandon our false god and embrace Him fully? It is when we abandon our created god and embrace the Creator God of love and mercy, that we are truly transformed and ready to serve Him. Did Jonah ever reach that transforming moment in his life? Let the reader decide.

ACKNOWLEDGMENTS

I would like to acknowledge the sailors and Marines I lived and sailed with across the oceans of the world. These strong, tough, and sometimes rough souls were, at the same time, capable of great acts of kindness, self-sacrifice, and spirituality. They taught me, their chaplain, many valuable lessons about the wideness of God's mercy.

My thanks also goes to my beloved wife Ruth, of 54 years, whose love, wise counsel, commitment, and collaboration on this work helped bring it to reality.

WHO IS THIS SON OF AMATTAI?

The book of Jonah is one of the great little books of the Old Testament. So valuable is it for us today, that the Holy Spirit let it spill over into the New Testament and into the teaching of Christ himself. Yet, it has been a book of much controversy in the Church. The more liberal interpreters tend to dismiss the book as just more myth, fable, or fairy tale because of the great fish which swallowed the prophet. On the other hand the more conservative interpreters want to make the book a test of orthodoxy. If you believe the whole story you are orthodox; but if you deny the story about the fish, then your faith is in question. But what about the Jewish Community? They list it among their minor prophets in their scriptures. In addition they read it every year during Yom Kippur, the Day of Atonement to remind them that God does seek salvation for the whole world, and not just for Israel alone.

Islam also embraced the account of Jonah and point to his tomb which they believe is located in the nation of Iraq. However, recently it was desecrated by Islamic radicals who had invaded the area. Christ made reference to Jonah's visit and subsequent deliverance from the fish's belly as a picture of His own life and time in the tomb and His subsequent resurrection on the third day. Jesus spoke of the "sign of Jonah" which we will discuss later in the book.

The book of Jonah is probably the most Christian book in the Old Testament because it deals with the love and mercy that would be shown us later in Christ. It is also unique because it, unlike other prophetical books, does not focus on the <u>message</u> of the prophet so much as it focuses on the prophet's personal <u>response</u> to God's message. Finally, the book expresses a subtle humor which the reader should not miss. The validity of the book is an easy call for this writer. Its message; its insights into God, the prophet and the Ninevites; as well as it's affirmation by Jesus in the Gospels, in the writer's judgment, makes it a divinely-inspired treasure for this generation.

The Two Gods in Jonah's Life

The Book of Jonah holds many powerful lessons for the Church and nations today. We have time to focus on but a few. Patrick Morley, in his book <u>The Seven Seasons of a Man's Life</u>, makes a profound observation about some Christians today. He said, "There is the God we want and the God who is…they are often not the same [God]. The great transformational point of our lives is when we see this and begin to seek the God who is and not the God we want." Let that sink in. It can turn your life upside down. It did so to Jonah.

In the April, 2011, edition of the magazine, "Christianity Today", theologian Miroslav Volf was asked, "Do Muslims and Christians worship the same God?" To which he replied, "First, all Christians do not worship the same God, and all Muslims do not worship the same God." Volf's insight was profound! The God people want, worship, and serve, can vary widely from the God who actually is. This is why, as we examine Jonah, we find Jonah examining us. We must keep glancing over our shoulder to see if the shadow of the great fish is stalking us.

The Complexity of Jonah

Who was Jonah and Who was the God he wanted to serve? Jonah was from Gath-Hefer, a village in the Northern Kingdom of Israel, only a day's journey from where Jesus grew up in Nazareth. The time is thought to be somewhere between 800 and 750 BC. If he is the same Jonah mentioned in II Kings 14:25ff who served under King Jeroboam II, he may have been an important counselor or advisor to the government. Since he became a prophet during the time of Elisha, he could have been trained and mentored by him, perhaps even to be his successor. So there is some evidence that Jonah was already a respected, historical, religious figure in Israel. This may account for why God chose him for this important mission to Nineveh. He loved and revered the God of the Jews; the God who had chosen him to be an Israelite, to share in the sacred Covenant, to worship in the Holy Temple at Jerusalem, and to celebrate the nation's holy days and festivals and seasons that belonged uniquely to the Jewish calendar. Jonah loved his people, his land, his religion, and his Jewish God. This was the God he wanted, with whom he felt comfortable, and enjoyed serving and proclaiming to his people.

NINEVAH!

The Call that Challenged His Idea of God

Then one day God burst his bubble. He blew Jonah's yamaka right off his head and turned his comfortable world upside down. God did this by speaking just 20 words," Arise, go to Nineveh, that great city, and call out against it, for their evil has come up before me."(Jonah 1:2) We are not told how these words came to Jonah, whether by vision or by dream or by audible voice, but these words burst like bomb shells on Jonah's peaceful world and he would never be the same. This would prove to be the opportunity for Jonah's transformational moment.

Does Jonah suspect that the message of judgment he is asked to convey may, in the end, turn into mercy? How could God care about Ninevite terrorist? How could He ask Jonah to leave his own land and people and go minister to these "animals"? Bloody Nineveh, as some called it, was the capital of Assyria and lay about 750 miles northeast of Israel. Jonah, as a true Israelite, hated Assyrians. Their reputation for bringing untold suffering upon Jonah's people was renowned. When they made forays into the Northern Kingdom, they stole their crops and cattle, burned their homes and towns, cut off hands and feet, dashed their children's heads against the stones, and took their wives and daughters for their sensual pleasures. Israel had been forced to pay them tribute, tribute that no doubt went to help build and maintain that wicked and bloody city of Nineveh. How could a just God care about such monsters?

Has God gone crazy? Jonah has his standards. He is prepared to forsake his sacred calling rather than stoop to participating in an act of mercy toward the Assyrians. Jonah's God exists to care for the needs of His people, the Hebrews. His mercy is to extend over the nation of Israel but must stop at its borders. We might ask, "How could Jonah, a prophet of God, a holy man, arrive at such a wrong-headed idea of God? How could he be so close to God and yet so far away?"

Jonah is Not Alone

Consider Judas, one of Jesus' twelve. He loved and followed the Jesus he wanted. Judas sacrificed much for Jesus. He spent many a night sleeping on the hard ground, eating cold sandwiches, washing his socks and underwear in streams and missing his family. He was dedicated to

Jesus, at least the Jesus he wanted Him to be. But when Jesus began to ask His disciples to love, to minister to, and to sacrifice their lives for the world and the worst, as He was prepared to do, Judas said, "NO! Absolutely not! This is not the Jesus I want or signed on with," and he rose up, like Jonah, to flee from His presence.

Consider Mohammed. He was a religious man who knew about the Christian God (Jehovah) the God who was. But, for whatever reason, he chose a different god while praying in a dark mountain cave. He was told by a voice that the Christian scriptures were in error, that Jesus was not God's only begotten son, and that He did not die on a cross for poor lost souls. The voice told him that the true god and his plan would be revealed to Mohammed and he would become this god's true prophet. So, Mohammed chose the god he wanted over the God who was and there are now approximately 3 billion Muslims today.

Another man, Joseph Smith, from Vermont, moved to New York, looking for the god he wanted. Upon his arrival in New York, he found the state in the middle of a great spiritual awakening. People were repenting, churches were coming alive to God and His word, and thousands of burning hearts were being swept into the kingdom of God. But, Joseph Smith had his own ideas about the god he wanted and it was not the God who was sweeping across New York State. So, he testified that he met an angel who told him that this work of God going on in New York was in error and that their churches and their Bible were in error. As a result, Joseph Smith chooses another god, the god he wanted. Rejecting the God of the historical Bible, the God of the Great Awakening burning across New York, the God of our Christ, and the work of His Holy Spirit, Joseph Smith embraced a different god. This god, according to Joseph Smith, designated him as his true prophet and leader of a new religious movement for latter day saints. His Mormon followers now number in the millions today. We see, then, that Jonah's thinking casts a long shadow and is probably found, in some manner, in every religious community.

But how about us? Can the same thing be happening to us without us knowing it? Are we serving the God who is or the god we want? If they are not the same, like Jonah we too may be headed for a crisis in the fish's belly.

Notes & Reflections

THE CRISIS THAT EXPOSED HIS FLAWS

Jonah's response to God's command to go to Nineveh, the great city, is recorded in these words, "But Jonah arose to flee to Tarshish, from the presence of the Lord. He went down to Joppa, and he found a ship going to Tarshish. So he paid the fare and went down into it to go with them to Tarshish, away from the presence of the Lord." (Jonah 1:3) How could Jonah, an Israelite who knew that God was everywhere, think that he could flee from Him? The answer must be in self delusion, a delusion that is wide-spread still today. We have often been reminded that when Jonah began to flee from the Lord, his direction was always down. One wonders if Jonah had ever read Psalm 139:7: "Where shall

I go from your Spirit? Or where shall I flee from your presence? If I ascend to heaven, you are there! If I make my bed in Sheol, you are there! If I take the wings of the morning and dwell in the uttermost parts of the sea, even there your hand shall lead me, and your right hand shall hold me." Joppa was a sea port on the northern coast. Here Phoenician ships sailed to all parts of the Mediterranean. Jonah found a ship bound for Tarshish, a city at the far end of the Mediterranean Sea, facing the Atlantic Ocean. It was considered to be at the other end of the world, about 1,500 miles from Israel and some 2,000 miles from Nineveh. Ancient Tarshish was located in what is now Spain. Near here Lord Nelson and his Royal Fleet, fought the famous battle of Trafalgar, defeating the French Navy and writing himself into English history. A monument to this famous sea battle and its admiral stands prominently in the center of London. Jonah, however, would never see Trafalgar because his great sea battle would be fought just off the coast of Israel. Let all beware who think they can escape God. God's "GPS" is always on and his "Smart Bombs" or storms can reach us anywhere.

Jonah is Introduced to a Pagan Culture

People on the run tend not to talk much. Jonah quietly and quickly bought his ticket, boarded the ship, went below deck to his assigned bunk and lay down to rest. Fleeing from God is usually exhaustive. It can wear you out physically, mentally and emotionally. As he rests he can hear the pagan sailors loading cargo and cursing as they work. Their language tells him that he is now in a culture definitely not Hebrew and this ship is far from the smells and bells of the Holy Temple.

The vessel is finally loaded and the Captain's voice can be heard ordering his crew to "Cast off the bow line and cast off the stern line. The ship is underway!" These are the words Jonah has longed to hear. The prophet is both relieved and uneasy as he feels the ship slowly swaying beneath him as the sails are lifted and it makes its way toward the breakwater and the open sea. So far so good. The ship sails past smaller boats where fishermen are busily pulling and repairing their nets. As the ship sails into deeper water the swells begin to increase, rocking the ship back and forth. Soon the tired prophet is sound asleep. But what the disobedient prophet cannot see from his dark hammock deep in the bowels of the ship are the large, mysterious black clouds quickly forming on the horizon, directly in the ship's path. They seemed to come out of nowhere but now have the full attention of the Captain. Such storms regularly claimed small, heavily loaded and vulnerable ships like his.

The Center of the Storm.

First the clouds appear, then the winds increase, quickly turning the once-calm sea into white caps; powerful waves begin to pound hard against the ship's hull until they threaten to break the vessel apart. The Israelites believed that the winds were God's servants. Psalm 104:3-4 says that He makes the clouds His chariots and rides upon the wind and makes the wind His messengers. It is clear now that this is no ordinary storm. There is something strange about its sight and fury. The cursing sailors struggle to stand and to secure the ship and its cargo against the storm. The account says," ...the Lord hurled a great wind upon the sea, and there was a mighty tempest on the sea."(1:4) As things rapidly deteriorate the sailors are ordered to start throwing the cargo over the side to lighten the ship but even this does not help. Next, the Captain, knowing that the ship and all aboard are in grave danger, checks his ship's holds for passengers and he finds Jonah fast asleep in the bottom of the ship. This both astounds and angers the Captain.

Notes & Reflections

HOW TO FALL FROM PROPHET TO FISH BAIT

When a ship is in danger all aboard are expected to be up and ready to lend a hand. The upset Captain awakens Jonah and reprimands him. He knows Jonah probably has no seamanship skills to offer but he demands that he at least pray to his god for the safety of the ship and crew. The prophet is scorned and rebuked by the pagan Captain for neglecting his religious duties. This should have pierced his conscience, embarrassing and humiliating him. As conditions worsen, the pagan sailors turn the ship into a house of prayer, each crying out to his own god for deliverance and mercy. What a surprise this must have been to Jonah, that these cursing, crude, pagan, sailors were capable of such a sincere, spiritual response, especially when his own heart is so cold.

This teaches us that we must be careful judging who is capable of spiritual response and who is not. We just might be the one standing in the need of prayer. God is teaching Jonah and us some profound things about Himself and others in this storm. What is Jonah learning about Nineveh by observing these sailors? What is he learning about the futility of trying to escape God? The sailors come to understand that there must be some relationship between the storm and this stranger on board. They begin to pepper him with questions, "Who are you, where did you come from, what have you done?" Jonah confesses he is a Prophet of the God who made the sea and land but he doesn't tell them what he has done to bring this judgment upon them all. For now, he will keep his dark secret hidden from them. Notice also that his description of God has to do more with His creative side than with His nature of judgment and compassion. The sailors want to know more and ask him out right, "What is this that you have done?"(1:10) Jonah continues to avoid a true confession. They now ask him," What shall we do to you that the sea may quiet down for us." (1:11) "Pick me up and hurl me into the sea... for I know it is because of me that this great tempest has come upon you", he replies. (1:12)

Sailors have a long history of throwing people overboard who offend them. It was not against their values, but in this case they feel compelled to show Jonah amazing mercy and grace. They choose to delay their "prophet-pitching party" until they try once again to save the ship lest they offend Jonah's God. But, try as they might, God wins the battle and they finally submit to His power in the storm and toss Jonah over the side.

Now, we may ask, why didn't Jonah simply jump over the side? Some argue that suicide would have violated his religious beliefs. However, King Saul and Samson, two Israelite leaders, both committed suicide. It could have been that he was unwilling to voluntarily sacrifice his life for the pagan sailors. It is the writer's judgment that Jonah is a coward.

In the Midrash literature, which is a body of exegesis material commenting on the Torah, written by Jewish sages, a writer addresses Jonah's being tossed into the sea. Midrash writers often tell stories to fill in the gaps where scripture is silent. One writer describes the pagan sailors' reluctance to toss Jonah fully into the sea by picturing them letting him over the side a little at a time while checking the status of the storm. First, they place his feet in the sea, then they lower him up to his knees, then to his waist, and then to his neck. When the storm does not subside they finally lower him completely into the water and he is gone. Immediately the raging storm ends and they find themselves in eerie quietness. One would like to have heard the conversations of the sailors following this incident. However, it says, "The men feared the Lord exceedingly, and they offered a sacrifice to the Lord and made vows" (1:16). Does this not describe their new-found faith in the living God? Amazing! Next, the scene shifts back to Jonah.

Enter the Great Fish

Sinking like a rock, Jonah holds his breath in sheer panic; preparing to meet his God and Day of Judgment. Then, suddenly he senses the sound and pressure of the rushing sea as a mighty fish from God's creative hand bears down upon him with its mouth wide open. Jonah's world spins as he is sucked down its slimy gullet. Tumbling downward, he can hear the beast's heart pounding like a giant drum and he can hear the swishing and gurgling of its bodily fluids about him like a working chemical factory. In a moment's time Jonah plunges headlong into the fish's stomach, a gooey swimming pool of digestive juices, and bubbling, burning stomach acid. It's a dark, putrid cesspool which he now shares with random pieces of half-digested squid, fish, and sea weed. The prophet who would flee from God and his sacred calling has now been reduced to, of all things, fish food! Jonah finds himself imprisoned in a hell from which he cannot escape. Hemmed in by the bars of the fish's mighty ribs, he is held captive at the bottom of the sea and nobody knows where he is - except God!

Dwight L. Moody, the famous American Evangelist, often said that if one could send all young preachers to hell for a time, they would all return better preachers. God is trying to make a better preacher out of Jonah, a preacher who will share His heart, purpose, and passion for souls. Half-stunned, Jonah examines his surroundings. He is a broken and terrified man, a lost prophet, no longer able to flee from God. One cannot help but compare Jonah's experience in the fish's belly with that of the rich man who died in Jesus' story found in the Gospel of Luke, chapter 16. Here, the rich man died and awoke in hell and, like Jonah, had no trouble praying in his affliction. (Luke 16:22-24) It is sad, is it not, that it will take hell to get some folk to earnestly pray. But beware of "fox-hole- religion", it is not always what it seems to be. In our fears, we are often too ready to do what we need to do to escape, but promises made under such duress can quickly dissipate when things improve. It is written that Jonah lifted up his voice and prayed to God and God heard him. But it does not say that God was pleased with him. The good news is that God was present in the fish's belly, listening to his disobedient child. Although the prophet acknowledges God's mercy and grace in the prayer, we must be careful not to declare the work of God complete in Jonah:

> I called out to the Lord, out of my distress, and he answered me; out of the belly of *Sheol I cried, and you heard my voice. For you cast me into the deep, into the heart of the seas, and the flood surrounded me; all your waves and your bellows passed over me. Then I said 'I'm driven away from your sight; yet I shall look again upon your holy temple. The waters closed in over me to take my life; the deep surrounded me; weeds were wrapped around my head at the roots of the mountains. I went

> down to the land whose bars closed upon me forever; yet you brought up my life from the pit, O Lord my God, when my life was fainting away, I remembered the Lord, and my prayer came to you, into your holy temple. Those who pay regard to vain idols forsake their hope of steadfast love. But I with the voice of thanksgiving will sacrifice to you ; what I have vowed I will pay. Salvation belongs to the Lord!"(2:2-9)

Let us consider this prayer: Notice that praise is present. Worship is present. Thanksgiving is present. Sacrifice is present. Vows are present. God's sovereignty over our salvation is acknowledged. So what is lacking in this prayer? The central element missing is a clear statement of repentance! Jonah says, "Salvation is of the Lord!" True! But can there be salvation without repentance? I think not. So, was Jonah truly converted in the fish's belly? Does he now fully embrace God's heart and purpose? This question will have to be answered in the events still to unfold. It does seem that sometimes God will settle for half a heart with the expectation of getting the rest later.

*Sheol was a dark, deep place, somewhere below the sea, as opposed to Heaven which was light and above.

LORD, RELEASE ME AND I WILL KEEP MY VOW!
T. Cook

HOW TO RISE FROM FISH VOMIT TO PROPHET AGAIN

Next, God speaks to the great fish rather than to Jonah and after three days and nights the fish vomits up Jonah. At least someone is now listening to God. Suddenly the fish empties his stomach and Jonah is released from his prison. But is he really free? Is he radically changed? Is he a new man, after God's own heart or is he still clinging to the god he wants? Unless he is radically changed, is he qualified to go to Nineveh? It has been said that God sometimes uses a crooked stick to draw a straight line. As Jonah crawls slowly up the beach, shading his eyes from the bright sun, he is grateful to be alive but does he still resemble a crooked stick? How will he ever be able to tell his wife and friends what has happened to him? It is worth noting that God pins no purple heart on his chest; He gives him no hero's welcome or ticker tape parade. With the background of the sounds of the crashing sea and the squawking of the sea gulls flying over his head, the voice of God comes again to Jonah. " Arise and go to Nineveh that great city and call out against it the message that I tell you." (3:2) Or translated, "Let's try this one more time." Jonah sets out for the city from which he earlier fled.

Preaching With an Attitude

We are spared the details of Jonah's long trip to Nineveh which must have taken one to two months at least. We are also spared the conversations he may have had with God along the way. However, we will discover from the events that follow that not all issues between Jonah and God had been resolved by the time the prophet reached the city gates. We now can confirm that God does use imperfect people to carry out his perfect plans. As Jonah approaches that great city of at least 120,000 souls, what would he have seen? Nineveh was located on the east side of the Tigris River in what is today modern Mosul in Iraq. It was a city protected by a large wall, eight miles in circumference, with 15 large main gates, each guarded by a large stone bull. Inside the city Jonah would have seen large and beautiful public buildings, ornate temples, and lavish palaces. The pride of the city was its great library and botanical gardens that dominated the landscape.

It was to Nineveh that her great warrior kings brought their soils of war to embellish the beauty of the city. The prophet Nahum (Nahum 3:1) called the city Bloody Nineveh and for good reason. These warrior kings returning from war also erected great mounds consisting of the heads of their captives. Other prisoners who were fortunate enough to keep their heads often lost a foot or a hand or their nose and eyes. This was the city to which Nineveh was prepared to take God's message.

He obediently does as God commanded him and cried out against the city: "Yet forty days, and Nineveh will be overthrown!" We can only imagine the fear and apprehension Jonah felt as he delivered his startling and powerful message. How will these tough, proud Assyrians respond to a Hebrew prophet with such a negative a message? Will he become a martyr in their streets? Will he be arrested and tortured? Will he be beheaded or made a public spectacle? Or will they receive his message as from God, repent, and change their barbaric ways? If they do repent, how will God respond? Will He change His mind? Or if judgment comes how will it come? Will it come from a foreign army, a flood, an earthquake, or will fire and brimstone fall from heaven as it had on Sodom and Gomorrah?

Jonah faithfully delivered his message across the city in a period of approximately three days. At first the people were probably just curious at the sight of the prophet and his message. No doubt some initially scorned and mocked him. However, as the message is repeated again and again, the crowd begins to take on a spirit of sobriety and fear, listening with remarkable attention and focus, asking one another, "What are we to do?" There is a strange, mysterious power that begins to grip the city as people start to pray, confessing their sins and weeping. Some are near panic. The entire city is being galvanized around the prophetic message.

Fertile Ground

Let us take a moment to consider why Jonah's message seemed to find such fertile ground. What was going on in Nineveh before Jonah arrived? Zondervan's Pictorial Encyclopedia of the Bible, Volume 3, along with other Bible commentaries, points out that Assyria suffered two great plagues in the latter part of eighth-century B.C. when Assurdon III was Emperor. If Jonah's arrival in Nineveh was during this time, he would have been preaching to a people already suffering a kind of judgment. Secondly, the events in their history had begun to move the Assyrians more and more away from polytheism toward monotheism. This might account for why it was easier for them to accept the message from the One True God. Also, the statement regarding their judgment uses the word "overthrow" or "overturn". This word would have gotten their attention. The Hebrew word for "overthrow" or "overturn" is the word NEH PACHET which is found in several Old Testament passages. It is used in Genesis, chapter 19, to describe the overthrow of Sodom and Gomorrah by fire and brimstone. It is also found in Job, chapter 28, verse 3, where it pictures a mountain being overturned, much like strip mining in Kentucky. It pictures a mountain being radically changed and transformed until it is hardly recognizable. A third use of the word occurs in Psalm 41:3. Here it pictures a sick man's bed being made. In the process we can imagine the mat or mattress on which the sick man lay being turned, shaken, and tossed, to restore it to its usefulness. This is a positive use of the term.

I remember as a child observing the turning and the shaking of the feather ticks to restore them to their usefulness. When I entered the Navy, it was not uncommon to see vessels in port with mattresses hung over the ship's lifelines in the sun and fresh air. They then would be turned, shaken and placed back on the ship's bunks. Although Jonah did not take the time to define what God meant by "overturned" or "overthrown", the Ninevites seemed to get the message: something radical was going to happen.

Jonah's use of the phrase "...in 40 days" must have also added to the sense of urgency. Forty days is not long! It precludes long discussions, debates, and delays. It is "Act now or never." In addition, in the Hebrew culture and, perhaps, in the Assyrian culture as well, the number 40 referred to a time of preparation to meet a divine expectation. Last but not least, there must have been a powerful atmosphere created by the preaching of God's Word. It is not unusual when God's Word is preached or read for the Holy Spirit to create a powerful atmosphere in, around, and among the people. This powerful presence of God cannot be explained as being the product of human manipulation.

What is important for us to understand here is that God had been preparing Nineveh for this day long before Jonah arrived. This truth still applies today and should keep any evangelist, missionary, prophet, pastor or lay person from claiming personal credit for the great movements of God that come to us

Fast Labor

The Bible says, "The people of Nineveh believed God, proclaimed a fast, and put on sack cloth, from the greatest to the least."(3:5) It has been said that Nineveh responded like a woman in fast labor. Before Jonah can explain how to do it she has done it.

There was a time when the writer thought all labor was slow and deliberate too. I remember hearing women tell how they had waited long periods of time for their children to be birthed. However, I received a rude awakening as a young pastor on my first charge. While in my study one morning I received an urgent call from a young wife in the congregation who was awaiting the birth of her first child. "I think this baby is coming now," she exclaimed in panic. "Can you take me to the hospital right away?" I jumped into my car, drove to her home, loaded her into the back seat so she could lie down, and headed for the hospital. However, when we realized I wasn't going to make it in time, I contacted the local EMT's who took over. She had the baby on the gurney as she was rolled into the hospital emergency room. Talk about a fast labor! We often think people cannot come to faith and repentance except by a long, deliberate process. Wrong! It can happen in an instant, like fast labor, when people are sincere and ready. We must be prepared to accept this pace of the Spirit's work and lend a hand.

The Ninevites were crying out, "What must we do to be saved?" The Holy Spirit leads them to embrace two basic Biblical requirements for any one to be saved: repentance and faith toward God. This is an amazing response considering that in the past the people worshipped many gods. Jonah's preaching is successful beyond his expectations, resulting in a true spiritual revival among the people. This sincere and radical obedience by the Ninevites can only be described as a wonderful work of God upon their hearts, from the least to the greatest. This is astounding, considering that in light of the events that follow, Jonah's own heart and attitude are unresponsive to God and the people.

The Response Spreads

In addition to their repentance, to show their sincerity and humility, they declare a fast and put on sack cloth. Even the King (whose name is not given), we are told, arose from his throne, put off his royal robes, sat in ashes and proclaimed an official fast with sack cloth for himself and all the people of the city, along with their domestic animals. Then, "Let them call out mightily to God. Let everyone turn from his evil way and from the violence that is in his hands. Who knows? God may turn and relent and turn from His fierce anger so that we may not perish." (3:8-9) Notice that this king does not guarantee that all will go well. He only hopes they will be spared. It was an act of unprecedented royal humility and submission to God. But why should we not expect religious revivals to include our public figures and leaders? Some of us may be tired of having our presidents say," I don't go out to church because it would disturb the other worshippers." However, we notice they do not have the same concern about attending a ball game and throwing out the ball. God never excludes public figures from their responsibility to repent and submit to His word also. When the famous Cane Ridge Revival came to Kentucky in 1801, it reached into its political and military leadership.

In the writer's extensive research on this city-wide revival, no information can be found among Assyrian records that mention this extra-ordinary event. This is perhaps not unusual. James Kennedy notes in his studies on Jonah, the Assyrians usually only reported military and political exploits and victories, rather than events that spoke about their humiliation, defeat, or religious experiences.

Nineveh's Revival Compared to Other Historical Revivals

America has experienced at least three major religious awakenings in its history and we have studied many others around the world, in such countries as England, Germany, France, Korea, China, Indonesia and South America, but none was ever as spectacular as this one in its depth and breadth. Not even Billy Graham saw a response like this, where a whole city embraced his call to repentance. Jonah 3:10 says, "When God saw what they did, how they turned from their evil ways, God relented of the disaster he said He would do to them, and He did it not." We do not always appreciate how willing and ready God is to hear and reach out to broken, wretched souls. This truth needs to be more clearly and loudly proclaimed from our pulpits and streets. Our failure to do so may cause many to succumb to unbelief, hopelessness and despair.

THE PROPHET DESERTS HIS CONVERTS

Our prophet is not pleased with Nineveh's repentance. The Scriptures say that," ...It displeased Jonah exceedingly and he was angry." (4:1) Notice the ever-growing gap between God and His messenger. While God is more and more pleased with the response of Nineveh, Jonah is increasingly angry with God and the city. The prophet is not about to call these new converts his brothers and sisters! He refuses to offer them encouragement, instruction, counsel, or discipleship training. Jonah is determined not to support the grace of God in this work. Things are now reaching critical mass between God and Jonah. As with Jonah, sooner or later God must confront our false ideas, false gods, and unworthy attitudes.

Jonah's Resistance Intensifies

Remember, Jonah had said from the fish's belly that salvation belonged to God. That is, God had the right to save who He wanted, when He wanted, how He wanted, and where He wanted. But now we see Jonah backtracking from his fox-hole declaration and complaining about God exercising His sovereignty. The next words out of his mouth are even more confusing and hypocritical:

> O Lord is this not what I said when I was yet in my country? That's why I made haste to flee to Tarshish: for I knew that you are a gracious God and merciful, slow to anger and abounding in steadfast love and relenting from disaster. Therefore now, Lord, please take my life from me, for it is better for me to die than live.(4:2)

We must give Jonah credit here for being honest about where he is spiritually. No one can come to God in faith until they acknowledge where they are. Here we see Jonah put one toe in the water, but is he ready for baptism? No! What kind of a man is this that accepts God's commission as a prophet and then thinks he can go his own way and expect God to meet his standards? Who is this man who confesses that he knows God is gracious and merciful and can change His mind yet steadfastly refuses to accept that change? We have to assume that Jonah is acquainted with the following passage in Jeremiah which set's forth God's declaration of His sovereignty. Here it is:

> If at anytime I declare concerning a nation or kingdom, that I will pluck up, tear down and destroy it and if the nation, concerning which I have spoken, turns from its evil, I will relent of the disaster I intended to do to it. And if at anytime I declare concerning a nation or kingdom that I will build and plant it, and it does evil in my sight, not listening to my voice, then I will relent of the good I intended to do to it. Jeremiah 18:7-10

If Jonah knows all this, then why is he angry? From the beginning of this account to the end, Jonah feels he is wise enough to counsel God. We laugh at such foolishness and yet it is more prevalent among religious people than we like to admit. When I was assigned as pastor to a church in a Seminary community I assumed that I would have opportunity to share my 30 years of Navy chaplaincy, pastoring and college teaching, with these eager young novices. Imagine my surprise when I discovered that these eager young students wanted instead to instruct me on preaching, church organization, outreach and worship. After only a few graduate courses they had contracted the dreaded and highly contagious disease we can call "the Jonah complex". This may be the religious Ebola of the Church today.

Jonah Deserts His Post Again

Next, Jonah shows his total defiance of God's compassion plan by departing the city without permission at the very time when the people needed him most. Jonah deserted the city and found a location on the east side where he constructed a booth, a temporary shelter from which he hopes to have a front-row seat to the destruction of Nineveh. Everything now becomes more and more about what Jonah wants than what God has ordained. It is worth noting that the booth is for Jonah alone. There is no room for others. He posts no office hours. Jonah is probably thinking about his reputation. He is keenly aware that the news of Nineveh's destruction would be far more welcome at home than the news of their repentance and, perhaps, a planned visit to the Temple at Jerusalem. In short, Jonah wants to see some fire and brimstone fall. It is worth comparing this scene of Jonah sitting alone, pouting in his booth, to the scene of Jesus weeping over Jerusalem. Jonah is demanding justice, not grace. But he hears only the sound of groaning and prayer coming from the city. What can possibly happen next? Surprise! God will again show grace and mercy to His unworthy servant.

The Gift of a Vine

"Now, the Lord appointed a plant and made it come up over Jonah that it might be a shade over his head, to save him from his discomfort."(4: 6) What? Disobedience doesn't deserve an act of mercy, does it? Will God's small act of mercy shown at this crucial moment awaken Jonah to his need of grace also? The text says that Jonah was exceedingly pleased with the plant. Oh, good! He does have some emotion left. God has constantly and patiently dealt graciously with Jonah in spite of his negative attitude. God did not have to save this prophet from the sea or from the fish. The Lord had no good reason to give him a second chance to redeem himself and go to Nineveh. He had no reason, humanly speaking, to preserve him from the violence of the Ninevites and He certainly had no reason to renovate Jonah's makeshift booth by covering it with a sheltering vine. But He did! God did it because He is, unlike Jonah, slow to anger and full of mercy. However, since Jonah apparently learned nothing from this act of grace shown him, God finally allows Jonah to experience a small taste of judgment that might eventually save him from the Great Judgment to come

The Gift of a Worm

The next morning God ends His small act of mercy toward Jonah by appointing a little worm with a ferocious appetite and strong teeth to bring down the vine of mercy. When the sun came up, the absence of the vine caused the sun to beat down hard on Jonah's head. The booth he built proved to be inadequate as will be the work we seek to do apart from God. A hot east wind is also sent against Jonah, scorching him and grinding the sand into his skin. Is Jonah again being sent a little taste of hell? I think so, but better to scorch a little now than to burn a lot later.

Jonah is growing angrier by the minute. Now he prays that God will let him die. He is so miserable, he would rather die than see the Ninevites live. There are people like this today. Our daily papers speak of radical terrorists who would rather die as a suicide bomber than see those they consider to be infidels live. In addition, Jonah's cowardliness is seen here again. He wants to die but he requests an "assisted suicide".

The Love of Vines Over the Love of People

"You pity the plant for which you did not labor, nor did you make it grow, which came into being in a night and perished in a night. And should I not pity Nineveh that great city in which there are more than 120,000 souls who do not know their right hand from their left, and also much cattle," says God! (4:10-11). God cares for people while Jonah cares for vines. Tragic!

In this penetrating statement the Lord reveals the whole purpose of the book. He is trying to overthrow the narrow, limited, and destructive view which Jonah had of Him and His relationship to the peoples of the world. Jonah sits alone in his small, crude booth of his own making, while opposing the God of the Universe's good and merciful work going on before his very eyes. Jonah was a picture of the whole Hebrew nation turned in on its self instead of outward toward others. Jonah's name means "Dove," but he had become just another selfish, angry bird parading in dove's feathers. Jonah's anger, his booth, and his plea to die reveal that he and God are now poles apart.

What Happened to Jonah?

At this point, God closes the book without telling us what happened to Jonah. Some say Jonah returned to Israel, wrote the book, and lived out his life as an honored prophet, being buried near Nazareth where the Savior of the world would later arise. Some say Jonah never made it home to Israel because God granted his request to die at Nineveh. Perhaps so. There is some evidence for this view near the old city of Nineveh. Here is located a mound called NEBE-YUNUS which means, "The Prophet Jonah". A tomb which some claim to be Jonah's exists near by. Recently the news reported that angry terrorists desecrated and tried to destroy what they believed to be Jonah's tomb. Jonah can't seem to find rest even in death.

A Word About Jonah's Mental State

A few words need to be said about Jonah's mental health. His strange behavior has elicited a number of speculations about this. Dr. William Bachus, a Christian psychologist, has written a small book entitled The

Paranoid Prophet, in which he uses a fictional psychologist to probe Jonah's emotional behavior which may have contributed to his anger and over-reaction toward God. Dr. Bachus has Jonah confessing to his psychologist, "To my twisted vision, God's mercy on Nineveh was as evil as my warning cry in the streets had been to my assailants—though that word I resented was God's own love sparing their very lives. I did not understand God's love and I thought it a weakness in Him." The author ends his book by putting words into Jonah's mouth that say in essence that God has forgiven Jonah and Jonah has forgiven God. Dr. Bacchus's book touches on legitimate struggles that are shared by many Christians today.

Dr. Shad Helmstetter, who works and writes in the area of human behavior, has a book entitled Who Are You Really and What Do You Want? Helmstetter argues that we need to do what he calls more "Self Talk" to know who we are and what we believe. Although the book is not about Jonah, its insights can help us to understand who Jonah was and why he acted as he did. Jonah seemed unable to engage in serious self-introspection. He was a rigid product of his culture, his nation, and upbringing. When God confronted him with new and greater knowledge of Himself, Jonah froze. His behavior causes us to wonder how willing we are to allow God to expand our thinking and behavior in order to conform to His character.

Had Jonah engaged in some introspection, he might have become one of the greatest prophets in the Bible. God offered him the opportunity to become a hero but instead he goes down in history as the prophet with the least concern for his congregation. Imagine what might have happened if Jonah had embraced the God who was, along with His heart and plan for the whole world. Think about what could have happened if he would have supported the revival instead of opposed it. We might be looking at a very different Middle East today. There are eternal consequences to our decision to embrace the god we want rather than the God that is. Think about that!

Nineveh Turns On Israel

Nineveh's opportunity never came again and neither did Jonah's, as far as we know. In fact, approximately fifty years later, Nineveh's Assyria invaded Israel and destroyed it, taking the people captive. From that point on, the ten northern tribes ceased to exist as a people group. Little did Jonah know that God's plan to save Nineveh was tied directly to His plan to save Israel. Here is a great lesson for all who are privileged to participate in any spiritual revival. Our responsibility is to discover what God is doing and fully support it as He gives us the grace to do so. By taking the Gospel of God's love to others in the world we actually help secure it for ourselves. Jonah was unable to participate in the Nineveh Revival because his god and heart were too small.

Who Was This Complex Man We Call Jonah?

Some would say that Jonah was the anti-prophet of the Bible. Certainly he displayed many characteristics that were not compatible with a true prophet of God. Perhaps some would go so far as to say he displayed many characteristics of the Anti- Christ spoken of in First and Second John and Revelation. However, we would have to argue that Jonah's life seems far more complicated. Along with all his weaknesses, we cannot see him as totally devoid of good. He does pray, he does give God credit for being a good and kind God, and he does deliver God's message to Nineveh. But who is he really? Could Jonah be that little worm that eats God's vine? It is certainly interesting that God places this little creature in the story at the critical moment when He is appealing to Jonah to change his attitude and join God's holy mission. Jonah would certainly not be the first or last "worm" that harmed or destroyed God's work, rather than built on it. Jonah either cannot or will not see the big picture God places before him. His god and his heart are far too small.

THE SIGN OF JONAH

Our study would not be complete without considering Jesus' reference to Jonah as recorded in the Gospels of Luke and Matthew, where he speaks of the "sign of Jonah". What is this sign and what did Jesus add to our knowledge of the prophet whose god was too small?

First, his comments from Luke 11:29ff:

> When the crowds were increasing, He began to say, 'This generation is an evil generation, it seeks for a sign but no sign will be given to it except the sign of Jonah. For as Jonah became a sign to the people of Nineveh, so will the Son of Man be to this generation... the men of Nineveh will rise up at the judgement with this generation and condemn it, for they repented at the preaching of Jonah, and behold, someone greater than Jonah is here.'

We should note that Jesus does not use this occasion to condemn Jonah or praise him. The "sign of Jonah" is not said to be his three days and nights in the fish, but rather that he preached God's word to that generation of Ninevites as Jesus was preaching God's word to His generation. What's more, Jesus proclaimed Himself to be greater than Jonah! Finally, Jesus says that these Ninevites who accepted God's word and were saved will stand up at the judgment and condemn the present generation of Jews who refused to hear Jesus' words to them. Secondly, here are His comments from Matthew 12:39ff:

> Then some of the scribes and Pharisees answered Him saying, 'Teacher, we wish to see a sign from you.' But

> He answered them, 'An evil and adulterous generation seeks a sign, but no sign will be given to it except the sign of the prophet Jonah. For just as Jonah was three days and nights in the belly of the great fish, so will the Son of Man be three days and nights in the heart of the earth. The men of Nineveh will rise up at the judgment with this generation and condemn it, for they repented at the preaching of Jonah, and behold something greater than Jonah is here.'

Again, Jesus neither condemns nor praises Jonah. This passage records Jesus' words about Jonah's three days and nights in the great fish and His own three days and nights in the heart of the earth. But what is the "sign of Jonah" here? We see again that Jonah preached, the Ninevites believed God, and they will appear at the judgment as witnesses against the unbelieving Jews. Again, notice also that Jesus is careful to say that He was greater than Jonah. So we see after looking carefully at the two texts that the primary "sign of Jonah" may not have been the resurrection of Jesus but rather the preaching of the Gospel, calling people to repentance. Sometimes we are tempted to embrace interpretations of scripture that may be popular rather than totally accurate.

It is also noteworthy that many see a remarkable resemblance between Jonah and the elder son in Jesus' story of the Prodigal Son, in Luke, chapter 15. By refraining from making the clear connection between Jonah and the elder son, Jesus may be yet again be extending one more kindness to Jonah.

Now, some additional observations on Jesus' comments concerning Jonah:

1. Jesus is silent regarding Jonah's aberrant behavior and salvation, probably because, at this point, this was not His purpose in citing Jonah.
2. The issue addressed by Jesus was the failure of His Jewish listeners to hear, repent and believe God as the pagan Ninevites had done.
3. Jesus was complimenting the Ninevites, not Jonah nor His listeners.

4. Jesus' comparison of Himself to Jonah had to do with their common experience in their call, preaching, suffering, death (or near death in the case of Jonah) and return to life, rather than a comparison of the holiness of their character. It must be noted, however, that Jesus does say that He is greater than Jonah. This, I think, says it all. Although they had some common experiences, in reality, Jesus and Jonah were miles apart in their embrace of the Father and His loving plan for the world.

Several who have studied the life of Jonah have found the English hymn writer, William Farber's poem, first published in 1885, most appropriate to the discussion of Jonah and his differences with God.

"There's A Wideness in God's Mercy"

There's a wideness in God's mercy like the wideness of the sea;
There's a kindness in His justice, which is more than liberty.
There is welcome for the sinner, and more grace for the good;
There is mercy with the Savior, there is healing in His blood.
For the love of God is broader than the measure of man's mind;
And the heart of the Eternal is most wonderfully kind.
But we make His love too narrow, by false limits of our own;
And we magnify His strictness with a zeal He will not own.
If our love were but more simple, we should take Him at His word;
And our lives would be all sunshine in the sweetness of our Lord.

God's generous love and mercy still stands as a rebuke to our narrowness, fears, and prejudice which we too often erect and allow to limit His grace.

CONCLUSION AND PRAYER

The book of Jonah challenges our tendency to embrace the god we want instead of the God who actually is. It exposes our partial and false surrender to God. The book speaks to the danger of living an unexamined life, which limits His grace to us and others. We need, as Patrick Morley reminds us, to understand why we think as we think, do as we do, and speak as we speak. Although Jonah confesses from the fish's belly that, "Those who pay regard to vain idols forsake their hope of [God's] steadfast love," (2:8) he fails to live out that confession himself. Where did Jonah's false view of God come from? It had been shaped on the anvil of his culture, race, religious experience, and national prejudice. This god had little resemblance to the true God revealed in Deuteronomy 6:4ff: "Hear O Israel. The Lord our God is one. You shall love the Lord your God with all your heart and with all your soul and with all your might. And these words that I command you shall be in your heart." Our true and only God demands a relationship with us based on a heart of love. Instead, Jonah offers Him a small, selfish heart of disobedience, criticism, obstinacy and anger. His behavior reveals clearly that he was not serving the God who was, but rather the god he wanted.

The story of Jonah challenges us to examine our lives and put away any idols we may have constructed either purposefully or through ignorance. We must then surrender our wills totally to the only compassionate and loving God Who is, so that we may become like Him. Perhaps this simple prayer can aid us in this transformational decision.

A Prayer of Surrender

"Lord, we know that we shall be measured, not by the position we hold or the church we attend or the nation of which we are a part, but we will be measured by the size of our hearts and the God we served. We remember Your words to us through Your servant St. Paul, 'I… urge you to walk in a manner worthy of the calling to which you have been called, with all humility and gentleness, with patience, bearing with one another in love….'(Eph. 4:1-2) Lord, we humbly repent of our own sin of rebellion. We confess that we have, like Jonah, allowed our prejudice, our narrowness, our race, our nationalism, and even our religious traditions and practices to blind us to Your compassion for the World. Forgive us, Lord; transform us, Lord; so that we can see past the small vines of life to the eternal souls of this world who are of far greater value. Lord, change us now, so that we may fully embrace You, Your loving, compassionate heart and plan for all people. We pray this in the name and in the spirit of our Savior, Your Son, Jesus Christ, our glorious example and friend. Amen."

ADDITIONAL QUESTIONS AND ISSUES WORTH PURSUING

1. What would lead Jonah to think he could flee from God?
2. Consider Jonah's initial relationship to the ship's crew.
3. What would motivate Jonah to be willing to die for the ship?
4. Discuss God's use of nature to get our attention.
5. Why does Jonah not seem to show fear of the storm?
6. Discuss why Jonah hid his sin from the sailors.
7. Where did the great fish come from?
8. Is the fish an instrument of God's judgment or of His grace? Or both?
9. Was Jonah's prayer from the fish's belly sincere?
10. Is there any evidence that the prayer might have been edited?
11. How might your prayer have compared or contrasted to his?
12. Do you think the fish was touched by the prayer?
13. How was Jonah changed by his experience in the fish?
14. Consider the kind of conversation he might have had with God on the way to Nineveh.
15. What emotions and questions might have flooded Jonah's mind as he entered Nineveh?
16. How do we account for Nineveh's quick response to Jonah's preaching?
17. What opposition might Jonah have encountered from the city?
18. Did God already know that Nineveh would repent?
19. Discuss where Jonah's anger came from.
20. How can Jonah describe God's compassionate nature and yet reject it?
21. Why does God continue to pursue Jonah with kindness?
22. Do you see Jonah as a likeable person?

23. How do you think Nineveh's citizens would have described him?
24. What did God mean by, "The people don't know their right hand from their left"?
25. Why did God end the book so abruptly?
26. Discuss why Jesus may have chosen to speak of Jonah in the Gospels
27. How do you think the Jews responded to Jesus' statement that the converts of Nineveh would condemn <u>them</u> at the judgment?
28. Why do you think we are more prone to want to discuss Jesus' resurrection in relationship to Jonah rather than our own failure to listen to God's Word?
29. Discuss why God sometimes uses imperfect people to do His perfect work.
30. Discuss how our imperfections can and do impact <u>our</u> message.
31. Do you think the Ninevites were able to separate Jonah's attitude from God's?
32. Why aren't people as prone to separate attitudes today?
33. Discuss how this revival might have transformed the Middle East, had Jonah and Israel given it their full support.

SELECTED RESOURCES

1. Achlemeier, Elizabeth....Preaching The Minor Prophets, 1998
2. Backus, William....The Paranoid Prophet, 1986
3. Bolin, Thomas....Freedom From Forgiveness, 1997
4. Briscoe, Stuart....Taking God Serious, 1986
5. Bull, Geoffrey....The City and the Sign, 1970
6. Craig, Kenneth Jr....A Poetics of Jonah. 1993
7. Desmond, David....Obadiah, Jonah, Micah, 1988
8. Enterprise Evening Star....Meet Orsen Whale, 2007
9. Gains, Janel....Jonah's Dilemma, 2005
10. Green, Barbara(Editor...Jonah's Journey, 2005
11. Henderson, Richard...The Jealousy of Jonah, 2006
12. Henry, Matthew....Commentary in One Vol., 1961
13. Hohluen, Richard....Translator's Notes On Jonah,2000
14. Kalodt, Ed....The Jonah Factor, 2006
15. Kemp, Bill....Jonah's Whale, 2007
16. Kendall, R.T.....Jonah, An Exposition, 1978
17. Kennedy, James....Studies in the Book of Jonah, 1956
18. Lacocque, Andre....The Jonah Complex, 1996
19. Lierk, Kenneth....Out of the Belly of Hell, 2006
20. McComisky, Thomas....Minor Prophets, Vol. 1. 1992
21. Moor, Johannes de....The Elusive Prophet, 2001
22. Morley, Patrick....Seven Seasons of the Man in the Mirror, 1995
23. Morley, Patrick...The Man in the Mirror, 1989
24. Morris, Tony....Jonah and the Whale, 1992
25. Nixon, Rosemary....The Message Of Jonah, 2003
26. Philips, Richard....Jonah And Micah, 2010

27. Rimmer, Harry….Jonah's Journeys, 2005
28. Soughers, Tara….Fleeing God, 2007
29. Wolf, Hans….Obadiah And Jonah(Commentary),1991
30. Zondervan Pictorial Encyclopedia Of The Bible Vol.3, 1975

CPSIA information can be obtained at www.ICGtesting.com
Printed in the USA
LVOW07s2237051015

456946LV00002B/2/P